GB

1/16

LEPRECHAUNS

KATIE GRIFFITHS

Cavendish
Square
New York

CREATURES OF FANTASY
LEPRECHAUNS

BY

KATIE GRIFFITHS

CAVENDISH SQUARE PUBLISHING · NEW YORK

Published in 2016 by Cavendish Square Publishing, LLC
243 5th Avenue, Suite 136, New York, NY 10016
Copyright © 2016 by Cavendish Square Publishing, LLC

First Edition

Website: cavendishsq.com

This publication represents the opinions and views of the author based on his or her personal experience, knowledge, and research. The information in this book serves as a general guide only. The author and publisher have used their best efforts in preparing this book and disclaim liability rising directly or indirectly from the use and application of this book.

CPSIA Compliance Information: Batch #WS15CSQ

All websites were available and accurate when this book was sent to press.

Library of Congress Cataloging-in-Publication Data

Griffiths, Katie.
Leprechauns / Katie Griffiths.
pages cm. — (Creatures of fantasy)
Includes bibliographical references and index.
ISBN 978-1-50260-500-9 (hardcover) ISBN 978-1-50260-501-6 (ebook)
1. Leprechauns. 2. Fairies—Ireland. I. Title.

GR153.5.G75 2015
398.2109417—dc23

2014049203

Editorial Director: David McNamara
Editor: Kristen Susienka
Copy Editor: Rebecca Rohan
Art Director: Jeffrey Talbot
Designer: Joseph Macri
Senior Production Manager: Jennifer Ryder-Talbot
Production Editor: Renni Johnson
Photo Research: J8 Media

The photographs in this book are used by permission and through the courtesy of: Wayne Anderson/Private Collection/Bridgeman Art Library, cover; Adams, Frank/Private Collection/Bridgeman Art Library, 2; Mary Evans Picture Library, 7; Fortean/Topfoto/The Image Works, 8; Steven Wright/ Shutterstock.com, 12; Hulton Archive/Getty Images, 14; Mike Kerrigan/Hulton Archive/Getty Images, 21; North Wind Picture Archives/The Image Works, 22; Brian Kelly/iStock/Thinkstock, 24; George Cruikshank/Archives Charmet/Bridgeman Art Library, 27; Олег Горбачев/Digital Vision Vectors/Getty Images, 28; Martin Fowler/Shutterstock.com, 30; Irish School/Private Collection/Bridgeman Art Library, 34; Nivasa/iStock/Thinkstock, 35; MCT/Newscom, 37; American School/Private Collection/The Stapleton Collection/Bridgeman Art Library, 40; Jangeltun/Digital Vision Vectors/ Getty Images, 44; Classic Vision/Age Fotostock, 45; De Agostini Picture Library/G. Dagli Orti/Bridgeman Art Library, 48; Charles Perrault, Harry Clarke (ill.)/File:Page facing 130 illustration from Fairy tales of Charles Perrault (Clarke, 1922).jpg/Wikimedia Commons, 52; Stephen Reid/File:Finn Mccool Comes to Aid the Fianna.png/Wikimedia Commons, 54; Kobby Dagan/Shutterstock.com, 59.

Printed in the United States of America

CONTENTS

INTRODUCTION

Since the first humans walked Earth, myths and legends have engaged minds and inspired imaginations. Ancient civilizations used stories to explain phenomena in the world around them: the weather, tides, and natural disasters. As different cultures evolved, so too did their stories. From their traditions and observations emerged creatures with powerful abilities, mythical intrigue, and their own **origins**. Sometimes, different cultures encouraged various manifestations of the same creature. At other times, these creatures and cultures morphed into entirely new beings with greater powers than their predecessors.

Today, societies still celebrate the folklore of their ancestors—in films such as *The Hobbit*, *Maleficent*, and *X-Men*; and in books such as the Harry Potter and Lightning Thief series. Some even believe creatures from these stories truly existed, and continue to walk the earth as living creatures. Others resign these beings to myth.

In the Creatures of Fantasy series, we celebrate captivating stories of the past from all around the world. Each book focuses on creatures both familiar and unknown: the cunning leprechaun, the valorous Pegasus, the cursed werewolf, and the towering giant. Their various incarnations throughout history are brought to life. All have their own origins, their own legends, and their own influences on the imagination today. Each story adds a new perspective to the human experience, and encourages people to revisit tales of the past in order to understand their presence in the modern age.

Beware the gifts
of leprechauns.

AN ELUSIVE TRICKSTER

"Lay your ear close to the hill.
Do you not catch the tiny clamour,
Busy click of elfin hammer,
Voice of the Leprechaun singing shrill …
Get him in sight, hold him tight,
And you're a made Man!"

WILLIAM ALLINGHAM, *THE LEPRECHAUN; OR, FAIRY SHOEMAKER,* 19TH C.

PERHAPS ONE OF THE MOST OVERLOOKED and **misrepresented** creatures in the world of fantasy is the leprechaun. You might have seen one first on a box of Lucky Charms cereal, but the legend of the leprechaun has existed for hundreds of years. Though many no longer believe in them, in past centuries leprechauns were believed to be real creatures that only a lucky few would ever see. They have been categorized as everything from elves to sprites to dwarves. This is probably due to the many different folklore sources that have combined to create our modern image of the creature. Regardless, today the leprechaun is recognized as a symbol of Ireland and of cunning, and has become a more prominent figure in the realm of fantasy.

Opposite: The leprechaun is the cobbler of the fairy folk.

The most popular image of the leprechaun comes from stories collected by **folklorists** in the nineteenth century. A leprechaun is usually a **wizened** old man, sometimes with a beard, who stands between an inch and a half and two feet tall. Female leprechauns are extremely rare in folklore, with some folklorists claiming that the female leprechaun does not exist. A leprechaun's clothes are both **aristocratic** and old-fashioned. Popular nineteenth-century images depict him wearing eighteenth-century fashion. In "The Elusive Elf," John Winberry describes the leprechaun's elaborate attire:

> His cut-away coat with flap pockets may be red or green and is adorned with a big, shiny button; beneath it is a long waistcoat. He wears knee breeches and white stockings, and his tiny shoes boast large, bright silver buckles. A three-cornered hat, on which he may spin like a top, usually completes his attire, but he may instead wear a red or green night-cap. Finally, a long, leather apron, like a cobbler's, covers his front. Stuffed into a big pocket of his coat is the leprechaun's magic purse, the *spre na skillenagh* (shilling fortune). In this little leather purse there is always a shilling, which no matter how often expended is miraculously replaced.

Each leprechaun has his own private treasure hoard that he keeps hidden somewhere in the Irish countryside. There are several theories about where this gold comes from. The most popular is that it is the remains of ancient treasure left behind by Danish **Vikings** when they raided Ireland.

Leprechauns are often portrayed as the cobblers of the fairy world. Although the leprechaun works for the fairy folk, he is often

in the human world—a leprechaun's favorite haunt is in shady hedgerows or in a clearing under a tree, where he will sit and mend shoes. Leprechauns are usually given away to watchers by the sound of their hammers or soft singing. They are often shown smoking pipes or drinking beer and Irish whiskey. While that image has changed somewhat in modern times, stories agree that leprechauns enjoy a chance to let loose.

In fables, the leprechaun is sought because he holds the secret of hidden wealth. The seeker will usually threaten the leprechaun's life in order to find this gold. However, the creature will do anything to avoid capture. Smart and devious, if caught he usually offers three wishes or gold to gain his freedom. However, he is crafty, and is known for using tricks to avoid giving away treasure. He can also disappear at will.

The creature has long been connected with good luck, particularly in the United States. In some pictures and stories he wears a four-leaf clover in his hat as a symbol of the luck he can bestow on whoever can catch him. In Irish tradition, the four-leaf clover represents the four ingredients for good fortune—hope, faith, love, and luck. Over time, the creature has become a symbol of Ireland and St. Patrick's Day, the celebration of Ireland's **patron saint**. Yet this is a long way off from where the leprechaun legend started.

Where To Begin?

The earliest known appearance of leprechaun-like creatures in literature occurred in Ancient Ireland. A tenth-century poem described *luprachans*, a relation of the modern-day leprechaun. Later, mention of another relative, the *lucorpan*, appeared in an eleventh-century book called *The Ancient Laws of Ireland*. These were "pygmy, dwarf or small

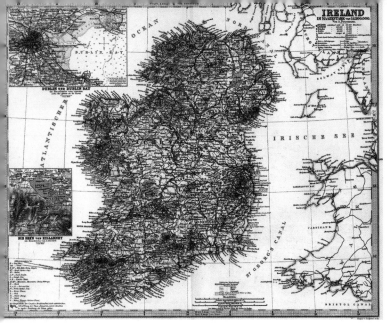

Map of nineteenth-century Ireland

gentlem[e]n." While seemingly always associated with short stature, it is clear that the image of the leprechaun did not begin as we know it today, but rather evolved over time.

Historians like W. F. de Vismes Kane have argued that leprechaun stories stemmed from **primitive** people's belief that magical beings existed in natural elements such as rivers, trees, and weather. These creatures were often described as "small beings living solitarily inside trees and prone to playing tricks." Others, such as Charles Squire, have argued that the creatures were a kind of **ancestral** spirit. It is thought that in Celtic times, people believed that when the soul was separated from the body it resembled a tiny person. The Celts believed that spirits continued performing everyday activities, such as feasting and hunting, even after death. Like leprechauns, these spirits lived in a mystical realm that could sometimes connect to the human world.

All But A Name

Ireland has long been associated with the origins of the leprechaun and persisting leprechaun stories. However, the word "leprechaun" was not universally used throughout Ireland to refer to these beings. In past centuries, it was spelt or pronounced differently in each region of Ireland. In northern parts, the creature was called a *logheryman*, in eastern parts a *lurikeen*, and in south and southwestern areas it was known as a *luaracan* or *cluricaun*; this has led to confusion and overlap between the leprechaun and its relative, the house spirit *clurichaun*.

Magical Little Men

While the image of the little green man with his pot of gold might be a symbol of Ireland, leprechauns, in their many shapes and with different names, can be found in stories all over the world.

For instance, in Hawaii there are the *menehune*. These two-foot-high creatures are always naked, but have long straight hair that falls to their knees and keeps them warm and covered. No two are the same shape, and they are said to be so tricky that they should be avoided, unless a special favor is needed of them. They are expert builders and craftsmen, and also very strong. They are fond of dancing, singing, and archery.

In England, the most famous legend is that of the Tommyknockers. They are found deep underground, in the old Cornish mines. They are two feet tall, green, and often seen wearing traditional miners' clothes. They are known for playing practical jokes, such as stealing unwatched tools and food. Their name comes from the knocking sound that is often heard before a cave-in.

In Holland, the *kabouter*, a Dutch word for gnome, is a tiny man who lives underground, in mushrooms, or in the home. They have long, full beards and wear tall, pointed hats. Most Dutch folktales about kabouters tell of the creatures teaching deserving humans how to make wooden shoes.

Lastly, there is the Swedish *tomte*. Only three feet tall, tomte are elderly men with long white beards and colorful clothes. They live secretly in houses and act as the family's guardian. If treated kindly, the tomte will protect children and animals from misfortune, and also help with housework. However, if offended, the tomte will play tricks or even kill **livestock**!

THE EVOLUTION OF LEPRECHAUNS

*"By birth the Leprechawn [sic] is of low descent,
his father being an evil spirit and his mother a degenerative fairy;
by nature he is a mischief-maker, the Puck of the Emerald Isle."*
DAVID RUSSELL MCANALLY, *IRISH WONDERS*, 1888

T HE TRUE ORIGINS OF THE LEPRECHAUN HAVE baffled writers and historians for years. They have been labeled at different times as dwarves, fairies, and sprites, though they are most commonly believed to be a type of elf or a hybrid of spirit and fairy. Depending on the century, they have been portrayed as everything from friendly household helpers to malicious baby-snatchers. Their dashing red coats and tri-cornered hats have, over time, been replaced with green jackets and bowler hats. So how did they develop and where exactly did they come from?

ORIGINS

Tracing leprechauns back to their roots has resulted in three main theories:

Opposite:
Leprechauns only bring help when they think the receiver is asleep.

1. The leprechaun was originally a primitive nature spirit.

2. The creature evolved from ancestral spirits that lived together in another world.

3. The idea of the leprechaun was a foreign influence by Danish invaders.

These theories have been explored and examined over centuries. Which one is correct, however, is yet to be determined. They all have weight and bring a more sound understanding of the origins of the leprechaun.

Leprechauns as Spirits

The first people to settle Ireland made sense of the world by inventing gods and spirits. For example, they believed in nature spirits, who they thought controlled the natural elements of their physical world. They imagined these beings to be very small—small enough to live inside trees—and to often play tricks on humans. The modern leprechaun still holds some similar features to these creatures. As well as his love of trickery, he is known for his woodland haunts, his **solitary** nature, and his frequent use of green clothing—suggesting connections to the forest and nature.

Primitive civilizations also believed strongly in ancestral spirits. The leprechaun's similarity with these spirits goes beyond size and lifestyle. In stories, the creature's love of tricks often plays a dual role. His pranks are also punishment for those who offend or mistreat him. Families who respect his autonomy, however, are rewarded. In ancient cultures, ancestral spirits fulfilled the same

function. Their job was to maintain order in the house by punishing unworthy family members, whilst guarding the whole household from evil. The color green was sometimes used during this time as a symbol of death, and leprechauns in turn were connected to death and violence by their darker nature as kidnappers.

From Foreign Lands

Foreign influences may have also played a part in the creation of the leprechaun. In 1826, the Scottish author Sir Walter Scott wrote a letter to the Irish folklorist Crofton Croker, claiming, "that the Leprechaun is a superstition of Danish origin." In particular, Scott linked the leprechaun to the **Scandinavian** *duergar*, a dwarf that guarded hidden treasure. They even share similar features—their small height, their underground homes, and their skill with craftwork. Scott's words were grounded in historical evidence. At the end of the eighth century Danish Vikings visited Ireland on numerous occasions to carry out raids on its coastal settlements. From 830 CE they established their own towns in places such as Dublin, Cork, and Limerick. They and their cultural practices were major influences on the Irish people for many years.

Earliest Mentions

The earliest records of leprechauns come from ancient texts. One of the sources, published in *The Ancient Laws of Ireland* during the mid-eleventh century, tells the story of King Fergus who fell asleep on a beach after a hard day of traveling. While he was sleeping, he was discovered by a group of water sprites. These creatures are named "lúchorpáin"—a predecessor of the word "leprechaun." They tried to drag him back into the sea with them. However, as

soon as they reached the water, the cold hit Fergus and woke him. Realizing what had happened, he immediately seized the three tiny creatures. They pleaded for release, and Fergus, realizing their magical powers, struck a deal. In exchange for their freedom, they would grant him three wishes.

The lúchorpáin were the first recorded incarnations of leprechauns, but it was not until the thirteenth century that stories began to describe their powers and appearance in more detail. The book also features the later story of "The Death of Fergus." Here the lúchorpáin evolved into the *lupra folk*, or the lupracan. King Iubhdan holds a great feast and boasts of the strength of his lupracan army. His chief poet, Esirt, mocks his claims and, angered, the king gives him three days to prove himself. Esirt travels to Fergus's court and returns with Fergus's dwarf, Aedh. The dwarf is both stronger and bigger than the lupracans. Iubhdan is then challenged to visit Fergus's court, where he is captured. When Fergus refuses to release Iubhdan, the lupracans bring plagues upon the court. Eventually they win Iubhdan's return by presenting Fergus with a magical cauldron.

In the tale, a lupracan is described as extremely small: "the close cropped grass of the green ... reached to his knee" and at one point a lupracan is dropped into a goblet where "upon the surface of the liquor that it contained he floated round." He is dressed in Celtic aristocratic fashion with a "silken shirt," a "gold embroidered tunic," and a "scarlet cloak." Lupracans are described as attractive with "hair that was ringletted ... of a fair and yellow hue ... and skin whiter than foam of wave ... and cheeks redder than the forest's scarlet berry." The lupracans even have women in their population with "pure white" skin and fair hair down "to their ankles." This more developed ancestor of the leprechaun is not yet the solitary trickster of modern imagination, but his features are beginning to show. The scarlet cloak would later be replaced with a red coat, and lupracan womenfolk would soon vanish, but their diminutive size, wish-granting and magical objects would remain. Even the magical cauldron seems to anticipate the leprechaun's pot of gold.

Stories of sightings often followed a similar pattern. The hero would attempt to catch a leprechaun in hope of forcing the creature to hand over his gold. One such story was recorded by the folklorist W. F. de Vismes Kane:

In the same townland (Lemaculla), James Dudgeon … told me that about the year 1850 he was returning home early one summer's evening, and coming to the ditch of a plantation he saw one of these little fellows with the red cap sitting beneath him in the "shough." He tried to catch him, but the loughrey-man jumped behind a tree, and peeped round it. Dudgeon chased him about from tree to tree for fully half-an-hour, he said, till tired out; so he wished him good-night, and left him grinning behind a tree.

The Modern Leprechaun

Fast-forward a few centuries and the leprechaun has now become a not uncommon character of film and literature. However, his appearance has changed. His flashy red coat and lacy cuffs have been replaced with a quirky green jacket and bowler hat, and his demeanor is usually a good-natured, approachable one. Why did this happen, and how?

By the twentieth century, many people of Irish descent living abroad came to consider Saint Patrick's Day a celebration of Irish

heritage. As a result, the leprechaun, previously an obscure part of Irish folklore, became a mascot for the commemorative day. Green, likewise, came to signify Ireland, and so depictions of the leprechaun left behind the classic red attire and replaced it with green. Over time, the creature's previously sinister personality also changed, to one of happiness and friendliness.

This change was also visible in children's entertainment. Books like Herminie Templeton Kavanagh's *Darby O'Gill and the Good People* (1903) promoted the idea of the jolly little elf. In 1959, Walt Disney Productions released a film version called *Darby O'Gill and the Little People*. It showed the hero in a good-natured battle of wits with leprechauns. After a series of humorous adventures, the leprechauns help Darby to get his true wish—not gold or riches, but to see his daughter happily married. By beating the leprechauns at their own game, and not seeking benefit for himself but rather for others, Darby shows himself worthy of their friendship and his own happiness.

The sweet and jolly image of the modern leprechaun has continued into the twenty-first century. One of the most famous is Lucky, the leprechaun mascot of General Mills's Lucky Charms cereal. His catchphrase, "They're always after me Lucky Charms!" points to old tales of Irish men and women who tried to capture the leprechaun. He is usually shown dancing, laughing, and jumping in a happy manner.

Yet modern stories have still not completely forgotten the leprechaun's darker origins. In 1993, the comedy-horror film *Leprechaun* was released. It starred Warwick Davis as the Leprechaun, and Jennifer Aniston in her first feature role. The story follows the fortunes of two families that fall foul of a sadistic leprechaun named

Lubdan. In an attempt to **retrieve** his lost gold, Lubdan kills anyone who he thinks possesses or has been in contact with his treasure. Even those who accidentally get in his way are given no mercy. Davis's character merges earlier leprechaun ancestors' abilities into one being: He can grant wishes, mimic voices, move objects, and conjure **illusions**. Likewise, his strength increases whenever his gold is with him. His actions are fuelled by greed. The one difference from traditional leprechaun stories, however, is that his weakness is the four-leaf clover.

Lubdan (played by Warwick Davis) is not your average leprechaun.

It's All In The Family

In the nineteenth century, stories of the leprechaun gave rise to stories of much darker cousins, the *clurichaun* and the *far darrig*.

In folklore, the clurichaun looks like a little old man, no bigger than a leprechaun. Clurichauns wear brightly colored clothing—mainly red—and hats decorated with gold laces. They are very easily offended and enjoy getting revenge. However, clurichauns could also be useful on occasion. It was believed that a well-treated clurichaun would protect the family's wine cellar.

A far darrig, on the other hand, was much worse. The name means "the red man" in Irish. This is because he is said to wear a red coat and cap—much like stories of the leprechaun and the clurichaun. In *Fairy and Folk Tales of the Irish Peasantry*, the writer W. B. Yeats described leprechauns, clurichauns, and far darrigs as "slouching, jeering, mischievous phantoms." Yet, it is the far darrig who most particularly likes "gruesome joking." His powers include voice manipulation and giving people bad dreams. He is amused by mortal terror.

Opposite: Clurichauns were known to plague lost travelers.

WISHES
AND WISDOM

Oh, there lived in old Ireland, a wee little man,
And he went by the name of a leprechaun.
A fairy shoemaker none other was he
And he had the power of wishes three.
UNKNOWN, *WISHES THREE*

THE LEPRECHAUN IS KNOWN FOR MANY things, but he is famously a symbol of luck and of Ireland. He is most associated with wishes and magic. His powers vary according to different stories, but they are always used for the same end—to escape capture and to protect the leprechaun's gold. These powers fall into two broad categories: tricks and illusions, and wealth and wish-granting.

Now You See Him...

It is said that if you take your eyes off a leprechaun—even for a second—he will vanish. Most stories of the leprechaun revolve around the creature trying to make the hero look away. The more

Opposite: Rainbows are thought to lead the way to hidden gold.

foolish humans will quickly fall for this trick and look away before they have even found his gold. However, often humans in leprechaun tales *have* heard of this habit, and the leprechaun is forced to try much harder.

In 1891, Patrick Kennedy published a collection of oral folktales that he had collected from different parts of Ireland. It includes a story from Edenderry called "The Kildare Lurikeen." A girl called Breedheen catches a leprechaun. She carefully keeps her eyes on him and demands to be taken to his gold. He insists he has none, but she ignores him. The leprechaun appears to give in and leads her toward the nearby Carbury Castle. But just as they get close, he screams in her ear, "Oh, murder! Castle Carbury is afire!" Breedheen jumps in fright and looks up to the castle. As she does, she loses her grip on the leprechaun. When she looks back, he has vanished.

In William Allingham's nineteenth-century poem "The Leprechaun," the hero meets a similar fate. The speaker catches a leprechaun at work. The leprechaun offers him a pinch of snuff powder from a little box. As the speaker accepts, the creature flings the dust in his face. Once the hero stops sneezing, he sees the leprechaun has gone.

The leprechaun can also use other tricks to distract its **captor**. In some stories, the leprechaun can magically rip the hero's pants, in an effort to make him drop the creature. He will also tell lies, such as that the hero's livestock has broken loose, or that his own sword is about to fall and kill him. But his greatest trick is the rainbow. In many leprechaun stories it is said that the rainbow points straight to the location of his hidden treasure. This is perhaps the leprechaun's cruelest joke. Rainbows are optical illusions—mere

tricks of the eye. Because of this, they actually move farther away as you walk toward them. As a result, it is not possible for a human to ever reach the end of a rainbow. The **symbolism** of this is very important. The leprechaun's gold is something that belongs only to him. The harder humans try to steal what is not theirs, the further it slips out of their grasp. It is a **metaphor** against greed and over-ambition.

Three Wishes

The leprechaun is as famous for his wishes as he is for his ability to disappear and hide his treasure. Traditionally, a human who captures a leprechaun can ask for three wishes in return for the creature's freedom. This pattern began with the first recorded leprechaun story, the *Echtra Fergus mac Léti*. Fergus was granted three wishes in return for releasing the captured leprechauns. However, the leprechaun is first and foremost a trickster, and taking the leprechaun's offer of wishes is a risky business. Leprechauns have the ability to twist wishes to their own ends. In stories, the wisher often makes a wish, which the leprechaun then deliberately misunderstands. However, there are a few exceptions. For example, one story tells of a boy who captured a leprechaun only to discover that one of his ancestors had been a leprechaun! Since he was "family," the leprechaun granted the boy his wishes without trickery, and the boy lived happily ever after.

The only way to catch a leprechaun is to surprise him.

The leprechaun is also known for his wealth. Some say it is ancient treasure left behind by Danish Vikings, and others say that it is the leprechaun's savings, collected from making shoes for other fairy folk. In addition, many stories tell of his use of magic coins. The leprechaun is thought to carry two leather pouches. One pouch has a silver shilling that returns to the purse every time it is given to a human. The other pouch contains a gold coin that turns to leaves or ashes after the leprechaun has given it away.

Leprechauns have long been thought to guard lost Viking treasure.

Leprechaun Morals

Leprechaun stories normally revolve around greed. Almost every one is a cautionary tale against attempts by mortals to get rich quickly, instead of through hard work. The leprechaun himself is a model of industry and thrift. He works very hard making shoes and looking after his money. The symbolism of the magic coins is important. In "Irish Legends of Buried Treasure," author Barry O'Reilly explains:

> The treasure is almost always impossible to get at ... The illusory nature of wealth and the quest for it is amply indicated by the tradition whereby gold is transformed into something worthless, such as leaves or dust, clay or bones.

THE LEPRECHAUN OF THE ISLE OF MAN

The Fenodyree (or *Phynnodderee*) is a fairy creature that is said to live on the Isle of Man, off the coast of England. He is covered in thick body hair, much like the menehune of Hawaii, and as a result does not wear clothes. In some stories, when clothing is offered, he complains that clothing is uncomfortable, or even causes disease! He is generally a helpful creature. He is known to carry out laborious jobs for deserving humans, such as moving heavy stone blocks or cutting huge fields of grass. He has also been said to herd animals and harvest crops.

The Fenodyree is believed to be a fallen fairy knight. Stories say that the creature was once a knight of the Fairy Court who fell in love with a mortal woman. In order to spend more time with her, he began to avoid parties at the court. One night he missed the Royal High Festivities of the Harvest—known as *Rehollys vooar yn ouyr*, or "Great Harvest Moonlight." The king was so angry that he put a curse on the Fenodyree. He transformed the fairy into an ugly satyr-like creature and banished him from the court forever. The Fenodyree could not die and so became a sad and solitary wanderer.

A question remains: does this creature exist? Some seem to think so. In 1926, one was supposedly photographed by a man named Gideon Whitfullington-Phorcast. Whether or not he actually did see one, however, is up for debate.

4

CLEVER TOM AND THE LEPRECHAUN

"And one time I saw a leprechaun ...
but he was more in dread of me than I of him."
LADY AUGUSTA GREGORY, *BELIEFS OF THE WEST OF IRELAND*, 1920

THE LEPRECHAUN CAN BE FOUND IN MANY stories, but there is one that has formed our main ideas of their personality and magical abilities. It has been retold in many ways but always with the same outcome. In most versions, it is known as "Clever Tom and the Leprechaun." One of the oldest published versions can be found in Samuel Lover's *Legends and Stories of Ireland* (1831).

The story tells of a man called Tom who was hardworking and hated **idleness**. He is described as follows: "Oliver Tom Fitzpatrick was the eldest son o' a comfortable farmer [and] he was as cliver, tight, good-lukin' a boy as any in the whole county Kildare." One day during a harvest holiday, he hears the sound of a hammer

Opposite: Ragwort plays a role in the tale of "Clever Tom and the Leprechaun."

31

clanging and finds a leprechaun working under a hedge. Tom sneaks up to the leprechaun and greets him with, "God bless your work, honest man." The leprechaun smiles and thanks him. Tom asks the leprechaun why he is working on a holiday and questions the creature about the jug of beer beside him. The leprechaun eventually tells Tom not to ask so many questions and chastises him for wasting time instead of heading to work. The creature almost tricks Tom into looking away, but realizing the trick, Tom stops himself and grabs at the leprechaun. He tries to make the creature reveal the location of his gold. The leprechaun pleads and whines that he has no gold. Tom gets angry and frightens the creature so much that he agrees to lead Tom to where his treasure is buried. When they arrive, the leprechaun points to a clump of ragwort and says that the treasure is buried underneath it. Tom has no shovel, so he takes off his red garter and ties it round the plant. He makes the leprechaun promise not to move the garter and runs home as fast as he can. When he returns to the field with his shovel, he finds hundreds of identical ragwort plants tied with red garters. The field is so wide he knows he cannot dig it all up, and he returns home cursing the leprechaun's trick.

Creating The Leprechaun

In this tale, the image of the leprechaun is solidified. The creature is shown as both a trickster and a victim. He is an ambiguous figure, neither completely good nor entirely bad.

In his better moments, the leprechaun is shown as hardworking and careful. The story begins with Tom busy complaining that too many people are "idlin' and goin' about doin' nothin' at all." But when Tom sees the leprechaun, the creature is hard at work making a new shoe, even though it is a holiday. The leprechaun even tells Tom off later for "idlin' away yer time here" when there's farm work to do.

The leprechaun does not enjoy company, from either fairies or humans. In the book *Irish Wonder*, which features well-known Irish folktales, Russell McAnally suggests that the leprechaun's solitary nature is because "he ha[d] learned the hollowness of fairy friendship and the **deceitfulness** of fairy femininity, and left the society of his kind in disgust at its lack of sincerity." Similarly, the leprechaun avoids humans because he thinks them greedy. While the leprechaun is not exactly a "good" fairy, he clearly avoids those he considers morally bad.

Tom's story also brings out a leprechaun's more mischievous side. When Tom finds the leprechaun, the leprechaun has a large pitcher of beer beside him. His drinking coupled with his dislike for socializing also makes him rather rude. He ignores Tom's questions, telling him to mind his own business and stop "botherin' [decent], quiet people wid yer foolish questions."

Human Error

In its oldest forms, the leprechaun is always mistrusted. He is said to lie and whine and trick. However, maybe what makes us most uncomfortable is how humans react to leprechauns in folklore. The protagonists of leprechaun stories vary from the plucky and hard-working golden boy to the crafty housewife to the lazy cheat, but one trait they have in common is their behavior toward the creature.

In "Clever Tom and the Leprechaun," the leprechaun ignores Tom's questions about treasure until Tom begins to get angry. The tale says, "Tom luked so wicked, an' so bloody-minded, that the

"onco frop went the little fellow with the
spring of a grasshopper"

This illustration from the nineteenth century shows how difficult it can be to catch a leprechaun.

little man was quite frightened." Tom changes from a good, hard-working man to an angry, violent one, just for the chance at the creature's gold.

Similarly, in *Irish Wonders*, McAnally tells the story of Dinnis, a lazy man who refused to work, and instead spent all his time searching under hedges for leprechauns. One day he finds a leprechaun and immediately grabs it. He calls the creature an "ugly little vagabond" and demands his gold or else, "I'll choke the life out av yer!" Dinnis is so violent that he "shak[es] him fit to make his head drop off" and "chok[es] him that his eyes stood out." Dinnis is clearly not a good man and the reader does not want him to get the treasure. In fairy tales the good are rewarded and the bad punished. However, in folktales, the leprechaun seems to bring out people's worst behavior. But is this the leprechaun's fault or the human's?

Sometimes even just the idea of a leprechaun can be dangerous. McAnally also mentions another story about a real-life farmer. His name was Paddy Donnelly. Everyone in his village knew he was a careful, hardworking man who never drank. Eventually, all Donnelly's hard work began to pay off, and he became quite wealthy. Unfortunately, people refused to accept that he was simply careful with his money and good at business. They believed that his good fortune was due to a leprechaun. This made them angry that Donnelly had not shared his "leprechaun gold" with them. McAnally uses human intrigue to explain this reaction. He says that our "love of wonder" is more pleased by magic than "the mere mortal causes of industry and prudence." By this, he means that nobody wants to hear a story about a hero who worked quietly and saved his or her money over time, so they invent other, fantastical reasons.

Good Rewarded

Despite all this, there are some tales of good people who meet leprechauns and are rewarded. This is usually due to their restraint and carefulness. Those who are polite, nonviolent, and do not interfere with the creatures are blessed with good fortune and wealth.

One example is the tale of "The Little Cobblers," told by a man called George Hale and recorded in *American Life Histories, 1936–1940*. It tells of the McGuiness family, who were very poor and starving most of the time. The husband, James, spent so much time worrying about his family that he fell sick and died. The widow was left to look after their five children. Being frugal and thrifty, the woman managed to get by, but she could never afford to buy

her children anything new. She patched up their clothes as best she could, but their shoes soon became ragged and full of holes. Winter was fast approaching, and the widow was very afraid her children would fall ill without shoes to keep them warm.

One night she had an idea. She knew that the leprechauns were cobblers—maybe they could help her? She knelt on the floor and in a clear, sincere voice, told the listening air of her plight. She felt certain the leprechauns would hear her. In order to show her appreciation when they arrived, she cleaned the house thoroughly and fixed up a little meal for them. She left two candles on the table and five little pairs of broken shoes and one old pair of her own on the floor. After this she went to bed.

During the night she woke to the faint sounds of music. She got out of bed and crept downstairs. When she reached the closed kitchen door she opened it a crack and peeked in. The candles had all burned out but the room was filled with a strange light. In the middle of the floor were six brand new pairs of shoes, surrounded by fifty dancing leprechauns. On the table, the plates of food were empty. She was amazed. Then she remembered that if she entered the room, the spell would be broken and perhaps bad luck would come to her. So she quietly shut the door and returned to bed. In the morning, there were the new shoes and marks of little feet on the earthen floor.

Widow McGuiness's ability to restrain herself and not interfere with the fairies was rewarded, as was her honest appeal for help. She was not greedy or violent, and did not take what didn't belong to her. In short, she accepted their help as a gift and not something she had a right to—unlike Tom and Dinnis, who saw the leprechaun gold as their right for capturing the creature.

TO CATCH
A LEPRECHAUN

Catching a leprechaun is believed to be extremely difficult. Not only do leprechauns avoid humans, but they are also known for their agility and invisibility. If they spot a person nearby, they will instantly vanish. In ancient stories, the only way to capture one was to catch him or her off guard. A human could find a leprechaun by staying alert and listening for the sounds of a hammer at work. If they were lucky enough to find one absorbed in mending shoes, they had to creep up quietly and grab it before the leprechaun saw them. In some stories, the creature could also be drawn out with offerings of food or strong drink.

Nowadays, creating a "leprechaun trap" is a popular St. Patrick's Day activity. Originating in America, where St. Patrick's Day is celebrated annually by people all over the country, leprechaun traps are some examples of how other cultures have influenced the evolution of the legend. A leprechaun trap can be made from a cardboard box, painted bright green, with some pennies or an old shoe placed on top. The theory is that the creature will be attracted by the coins or the shoe and will step into the trap to get to them.

Opposite: A leprechaun trap

THE APOSTLE OF IRELAND ST. PATRICK, BORN A.D. 372, DIED A.D. 464.

Serpentes et omnia venenata animalia ex Hibernia baculo Jesu expulit.

5

PAGAN PEOPLE

"The king was dancing with the queen, the princess with the prince,
And all the other fairies joined in an Irish dance.
A ceilidh band was playing as the moonlight shone,
They played the sweetest music, this band of leprechauns."
JOHN WATT, "THE FAIRY REEL," 2012

IT IS SAID THAT HISTORY IS WRITTEN BY THE victors. This means that those who win the battle get to decide how their story is told. This seems especially true in the case of leprechauns. These creatures belong to Irish prehistory and their image today has been mainly affected by the arrival of Christianity to Ireland. Their connection to a mysterious past can be seen most obviously in descriptions of their clothes. Leprechauns are forever being described as dressed in clothes from a different era. In their earliest appearances they arrive clothed like Celtic warriors. Moreover, even in tales from the early twentieth century, they wear the costume of an eighteenth-century **dandy**. Clearly, these creatures continue to

Opposite: St. Patrick casting out the snakes from Ireland

DESCENDANTS OF GODS

Leprechauns are thought to be part of one of the ancient Irish races, the Tuatha Dé Danann. The Dananns were a mythical ancient race that was believed to have lived before the first Irish settlers. They were the **descendants** of Danu, the Irish Mother Goddess of earth and harvests. A race of heroes, they were skilled in art, science, poetry, and magic. According to legend and ancient writings, the Dananns settled in Ireland around 1800 BCE. The Irish writer W. B. Yeats went one step farther, claiming that leprechauns were in fact the gods of the Tuatha Dé Danann. Others, however, think they were descended from a different human race living alongside the Tuatha Dé Danann, while still others assert the Tuatha Dé Danann existed only in people's imaginations and creative writings.

One thing is certain: it was only after the arrival of new religions that the leprechauns and fairy folk lost importance and were turned into "little people."

be connected with the past. In order to discover how leprechaun history might have been rewritten, we must trace this past.

DISPLACED PEOPLE

According to legend, leprechauns belong to the fairy family, also known as the "good folk" or the "little people." People have different ideas on how fairies were first created. The more ancient religion of Ireland, Celtic paganism, believed that fairies were nature spirits. They protected the earth and had respect for it, or else suffered consequences. People would offer sacrifices to these ancient deities to ensure a good harvest or to ward off bad luck. For example, they would make offerings to water gods by dropping valuable objects into rivers and lakes. As Christianity grew, fairies began to be seen more negatively. Some thought they were souls who had died before being baptized. Others believed they were fallen angels who were not bad enough to be damned, but not good enough to be saved.

Some historians argue that these "fairy people" were a real group of ancient inhabitants of different countries. Long ago, when a country was invaded by a new civilization, the conquering force would often exile the original population. As a new people took over the land, the others were forced to remote places to seek new homes. It was through this method that new civilizations could push older ones out of everyday existence. This exile created a pattern. An exiled people became seen only rarely. These few sightings slowly changed to myth, myths simplified into tales about local spirits, until eventually these "spirits" became national folktales.

The elusiveness and mystery surrounding leprechauns has shifted into new thinking about their origins. One theory is that leprechauns are the mythical versions of Celtic druids.

Pagan Snakes

If there is a victor in the history of Irish religion, it is Christianity. Between the fifth and sixth centuries, Christianity became the most powerful religion in Ireland. This was largely attributed to a man named Patrick, a Scottish slave who converted to Christianity and, after escaping his captors, went on to share Christ's message with local Irish people. He later became Ireland's patron saint.

The story chosen by these victors was the tale of St. Patrick and the snakes. While converting people to Christianity, one of the miracles he performed was to drive out every snake from the island. Scientists and historians have now confirmed that there were never any actual snakes in Ireland during this time. So what does this story mean?

The symbol of Druidism

The snake is an often-used biblical symbol. In Christian belief, it is usually associated with evil, temptation, and original sin. In one of the stories of Creation, it is a snake that tempts Eve with fruit from the forbidden Tree of Knowledge. Yet it is also a symbol for paganism. In this ancient religion, the image of the snake is known as the "Snake of Wisdom." It closely resembles the symbol of modern medicine—two snakes wrapped around a staff. It is the calling card of the Celtic god Enki. He was a scientist, a physician, a medical practitioner, and a seeker of truth. He was believed to have anointed the first druid priesthood. They later adopted the snake as their symbol.

In paganism, druids were not just priests. They were also doctors, historians, and poets. They were believed to be the keepers of spiritual and Celtic cultural wisdom. They were secretive and guarded their knowledge carefully. Most historians believe that the story of St. Patrick is not a literal tale, but a symbolic one. It is a narrative of conquest, of how Christianity drove out paganism by exiling druids—the keepers of Celtic knowledge.

This fresco in Germany shows the destruction of the Celtic druids.

Christian Rewrites

An old countrywoman once told W. B. Yeats, "Hell was an invention got up by the priest to keep people good; and ghosts would not be permitted ... to go trapsin' about ... but there are faeries and little leprechauns." This neatly sums up the attitude of the fourth-century Christian church to paganism—leprechauns were tolerated but only as a form of demon.

Stories of St. Patrick's exploits include his condemning of Celtic mythological creatures to the underworld—a symbolic act of physically driving out non-Christians. Leprechauns have been negatively portrayed in other areas of Christian literature. One example is the *Lebor na huidre*, written in 1100 BCE and based on the Book of Genesis. According to the text, after Noah and his family survived the flood, his son Ham mocked his father. God cursed Ham to have "unshapely" descendants, or more specifically, to sire "Luchrupain." This frames leprechauns as the ungodly offspring of a cursed man.

It is possible that memory of Irish druids influenced the Church's portrayal of leprechauns. The druids' connection with nature and the forests lent itself to a connection with former nature spirits, who were now reduced to demons that lurked outside the safety of the Christian home. Many fairy tales, even today, show the forest as a place where magical creatures, including the leprechaun, hide. The leprechaun's pots of gold can also be seen as symbolic of secret druid knowledge that can harm the unwary seeker. In the Middle Ages, belief in folklore and fairies was close to heresy, and people had to be careful not to display too much knowledge, for fear of being labeled a witch!

Connections

In tracing the history of leprechauns in Ireland, we find a story with several possible beginnings and more than a few rewrites. In attempting to understand this creature we must acknowledge the influences of ancient races—both mythical and real, fairy mythology and the political agenda of both a dying and a rising religion—paganism and Christianity.

The image of the leprechaun may have been first created as a natural being, but was quickly recast by Christianity as an attempt to demonize a minority culture. Similarly, the powers of the leprechaun—such as wish-granting—are often portrayed as both connected to the natural world and the demonic underworld. But when it comes to wish-granting who is the real villain? Leprechauns or humans?

6

BE CAREFUL WHAT YOU WISH FOR

"If wishes were horses, beggars would ride."

SIXTEENTH-CENTURY PROVERB

WISHES ARE AN IMPORTANT PART OF OUR everyday world. They can be as little as wishing for a bus to arrive on time, or as big as wishing for love and power. We use all kinds of objects and people for our wishes—wells, dandelions, stars, etc. We wish as we blow out birthday candles or throw coins into fountains. Dreams and wishes are a central part of who we are and who we want to be. They show our fears and desires, and seem to promise a simple solution for making our dreams come true. Likewise, wishes have powerful significance in folklore, especially in stories about leprechauns.

Opposite:
Aladdin and his magical djinn

The Power Of Wishes

One of the most common themes in stories is the "making a wish/ wishes coming true" motif. In stories, a wish is a supernatural demand made to a magical object or creature. It is usually given as a reward for a good deed, such as freeing a magical being from an enchanted prison. The creature that provides the wishes is typically a kind of genie. Often the prison is a commonplace object, like a lamp or a ring. Releasing the creature from this object earns the hero three wishes. Leprechauns, too, have the ability to grant wishes. Often, like other wish-granting creatures, the leprechaun offers these wishes in exchange for his release. It is freedom that wish-granting beings most want.

One such story is recorded in *The History of Galway* by Sean Spellissy. It is a legend that is used to explain how one great Irish family, the Donnellans, gained their wealth.

Tully O'Donnellan was riding home from Ballinasbe, or some other place, and it was raining, and he came to a river that was in flood, and there used to be no bridges in those times. And when he was going to ride through the river, he saw a leprechaun on the bank, and he offered him a lift, and he stooped down and lifted him up behind him on the horse. And when he got near where the castle was, he saw it in flames before him. And the leprechaun said, "Don't fret after it but build a new castle in the place I'll show you, about a stone's throw from the old one." "I have no money to do that," said Tully Donnellan. "Never mind that," said the leprechaun, "but do as I bid you, and you'll have plenty." So he did as he bade him, and the morning after he went to live in the new castle, when he went into that room that has the stone with his name on it now, it was full up of gold, and you could be turning it like you'd turn potatoes into a shovel. And when the children would go into the room with their father and mother, the nurses would put bits of wax on their shoes. That way, bits of the gold would stick to them. And they had great riches and smothered the world with it, and they used to shoe their horses with silver. It was in racing they ran through it, and keeping hounds and horses and horns.

Of all the "wish-granting" stories in the world, wealth is the most common desire. Money, gold, jewels, and riches are frequently requested. Most myths and fairy tales were created and told by ordinary people. As a result, their fears and desires over money often appeared in these tales. Heroes were often poor and ordinary, and their wishes were usually about making their lives easier and more enjoyable. However, there is a message behind these stories: that magical money can be unreliable at best, and downright dangerous at worst.

A Cautionary Tale

Most folktales that deal with wishes are very skeptical of magical wealth. Often, the moral of these stories is, "Be careful what you wish for." Wishes can go very badly wrong for a number of reasons. Sometimes the magical creature is a trickster who purposely twists a person's wish for the worst possible outcome. For example, wishing for a million dollars might result in your aunt dying and leaving you the money in her will. Other times, a wisher misspeaks and the creature takes their words too literally. In Charles Perrault's 1697

Wishes are never easy, as the characters in "The Ridiculous Wishes" show.

tale "The Ridiculous Wishes," a man is granted three wishes after agreeing not to chop down a tree, which is home to a tree spirit. He goes home to his wife and accidentally wishes for a plate of sausages. The wife is amazed when they suddenly appear, and the man quickly explains about the wishes. She is so angry that he has wasted his first wish that she begins to ridicule him. In frustration, he accidentally wishes that the sausages were stuck up her nose. Quick as a flash, the sausages become lodged in the woman's nose and, try as they might, the couple cannot remove them. Finally, grudgingly, they agree to use the last wish to remove the sausages. These stories of "wasted wishes" were a common way to teach people not to be careless with good fortune.

Leprechaun Etymology

There are many variations from which the word "leprechaun" might have sprung. Yet most historians believe that the word derived from the Irish word *lucharmunn*, meaning "pygmy, dwarf, or small gentleman." It is made from *luch* (meaning "small") and *armunn* (meaning "a hero, warrior, gentleman").

WISH-GRANTING AROUND THE WORLD

The leprechaun is not the only creature known for trading wishes for freedom. In different parts of the world, there are many examples of magical tricksters who will grant wishes upon capture.

The most well known is the *djinn* or *jinni*, a magical creature from Arabic folklore. This being is more commonly known in the West as a genie. In Islamic mythology, djinns are demons that live in a parallel world to our own. The Koran says that when the world was created, God made three thinking and feeling creatures—humans, angels, and djinns. Similarly to leprechauns, they are ambiguous beings, and the Koran points out that "like human beings, the Djinn can also be good, evil, or neutrally benevolent." *One Thousand and One Nights* was the first story collection where djinns began granting wishes. They are usually trapped in rings or lamps, and will grant wishes to the person who rubs the object and releases them. In most stories, a wish granted by a djinn will usually backfire. Even if the hero tries to be clever, he will never outwit the djinn, and often must use his third wish to undo the first two.

Another lesser-known trickster is the Brazilian *saci*. Exclusively male, he has many similarities to the Irish leprechaun. As well as his mischievous nature, he is always seen with a pipe and wearing a red cap. His cap is a magical device that allows him to disappear, reappear, and become invisible at will. He frequently plays tricks on local people, such as disturbing animals and souring milk. If a person can get hold of his red cap, the saci will grant the possessor wishes. Another way to earn wishes is to persuade the creature to enter a dark green bottle. Once inside, the bottle must be sealed with a cork decorated with a cross insignia. Captured, the saci is forced to grant wishes to his captor. When he eventually escapes, as he does in all stories, depending on how well or badly he was treated during his imprisonment, the saci will become a powerful ally or a formidable foe.

LEPRECHAUNS AND SOCIETY

"WHAT should I be but a prophet and a liar,
Whose mother was a leprechaun, whose father was a friar?"
EDNA ST. VINCENT MILLAY, *THE SINGING WOMAN*, 1922

THE MODERN LEPRECHAUN HAS MANY FACES. He is a sweet fairy, a troublemaker, a heritage symbol, and even, on occasion, a demon. His appearance and personality change depending on where his image is being used. That difference can be seen in his move from Irish mythology to mainstream American pop culture.

The Irish Leprechaun

Most people are surprised to learn that leprechauns do not actually make up a large part of Irish mythology. More importance is placed on characters from the *Fenian Cycle*. This is a collection of prose and verse that tells the story of Fionn mac Cumhill (also called Finn McCool). Fionn was a mythical warrior who roamed Ireland with his band

Opposite: Ancient Irish hero Finn McCool (center) with his warriors

of fighters, the Fianna. Tales about him were based on historical bands of landless young men in early medieval Ireland. According to legend, Fionn built the famous Giant's Causeway as part of his battle with the Scottish giant Benandonner. It is these stories that inspire patriotic pride in the native Irish people, rather than leprechauns, who are viewed by some as more of an overplayed joke.

However, Dublin does have its very own National Leprechaun Museum. It was built to celebrate and raise awareness of Ireland's rich mythological background. Tom O'Rahilly, director and creator of the museum, was quick to point out the difference between modern expectations and past tales: "Irish culture is famous the world over—even Walt Disney came to Ireland to look for leprechauns. However, not many people know the real stories behind the country's folklore."

It is clear that Ireland is proud of its cultural heritage, but also that it is tired of being largely defined by the leprechaun. Nonetheless, legends about the mythical creature persist.

The American Leprechaun

The image of the leprechaun changed radically as it crossed from Ireland to America. In the twentieth century, books, plays, movies, and Lucky Charms cereal contributed to the modern popularization of the mythological creature. Most portrayals of leprechauns in American culture today show one wearing green clothing rather than traditional red, and having a friendlier demeanor. In the twenty-first century, American representations of the leprechaun are either of happy, harmless folk, who are more willing to give away their gold, or of conniving, murderous creatures who take revenge on disrespectful humans. They can be found in all areas of American life, but particularly in film and sports.

American films such as Disney's *Darby O'Gill and the Little People* and the lesser-known *The Luck of the Irish* have portrayed the leprechaun as happy and social. His tricks rarely cause serious harm, and he can be befriended. In *Darby O'Gill*, the king of the leprechauns is genuinely concerned with Darby's safety and even helps him to escape the king's own trick. In *The Luck of the Irish*, leprechaun traditions are almost thrown out completely. The story tells of a young boy who loses his lucky coin. He quickly discovers that he is actually half-leprechaun—his Irish mother is a leprechaun who married a human. The coin was helping to magically disguise him and his family. As he searches for the coin, his appearance becomes more and more leprechaun-like: his ears become pointed, his hair turns orange, and he begins to shrink.

Leprechauns have also made regular appearances on American TV shows. One example is on *The Simpsons*. A minor character, O'Reilly the leprechaun, can be seen in several episodes. The only person who can see him is the character Ralph, whom he tells to "burn things." Here the leprechaun's trickster image is pushed all the way into a hallucination that has nothing to do with Irish culture and is most likely a humorous reference to the Lucky Charms mascot. Slightly more realistic versions of the leprechaun can be found in shows such as *The Twilight Zone*. In one episode, three boys catch a leprechaun and he grants them three wishes. However, the wishes backfire and instead teach the boys important life lessons. Although nearer to the truth, leprechauns are still used as a magical oddity to move stories forward. There is no apparent desire in these representations to explore Irish culture or mythology.

The leprechaun has even made its way into American sports. He is the official team mascot for two teams, the University of Notre

Dame's Fighting Irish and the National Basketball Association's Boston Celtics. The Notre Dame football team's logo shows a leprechaun in profile with his fists up, ready to fight. Sports artist Theodore W. Drake designed the image in 1964. The student section at the games is also known as the "Leprechaun Legion." The Boston Celtics also feature a leprechaun in their logo, which has been used since the 1950s. He carries a *shillelagh*, which is a cross between a walking stick and a club. Finally, leprechauns have even showed up in wrestling! Dylan Postl, also known as Hornswoggle, is a professional wrestler signed to World Wrestling Entertainment Inc. (WWE). He made his debut in 2006 wearing a leprechaun costume and using a shillelagh to knock out opponents in staged fights. Later, in 2014, Postl appeared in the movie *Leprechaun: Origins*. This was a revamp of Warwick Davis's original role as Lubdan the murderous leprechaun.

Modern Sightings

Yet sightings of the creature have not completely disappeared. Some of the most famous reports come from Carlingford, a town in County Louth, Ireland. It is here that two residents claim to have found a leprechaun's suit and bones, and to be in contact with the King of the Leprechauns himself. They even used leprechauns as a way to petition the European Union for protected habitat status. The area was actually home to a number of rare flowers and trees. In 2009 the area was declared protected under the European Habitats Directive.

Backlash

However, not everyone is happy with the leprechaun's multiple public faces. The mass media versions of the trickster have rarely borne any resemblance to the original Irish tales. Often they fall

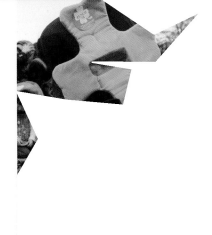

into two categories: The happy Disney fairy, or the angry drunk. Both versions have caused anger in the American-Irish community.

One of the biggest causes of the problem has been celebrations of St. Patrick's Day. The holiday is known for its energy, partying, and most importantly, its leprechaun images and costumes. But in more recent years, more and more St. Patrick's Day products have used pictures of leprechauns to portray the Irish as angry drunks. This increase has led some members of the Irish community to take action. The Ancient Order of Hiberians is the United States's largest Irish-Catholic fraternal organization. In 2014, they launched anti-defamation action against stores across the country. This meant that they could bring to trial companies selling products that used offensive stereotypes of Irish-Americans. In the lead-up to St. Patrick's Day, stores nationwide were selling T-shirts with slogans such as, "I may not be Irish, but I can drink like one" and "Blame the Irish for my behavior." In an e-mail to its then eighty thousand members, the Order said: "These items are an outrage to those whose Irish heritage traces to hard working Irish immigrants, not to a beer bottle."

A leprechaun at the St. Patrick's Day parade in Chicago, Illinois

The Big Picture

Leprechauns have sparked our curiosity for centuries. In their original form, they revealed our desire for magical solutions, as well as our caution of "easy money." They hold a unique place in our imagination, and their dislike of company makes them even more fascinating. While the modern leprechaun has lost some of his bite, his history and connection to Ireland's more mystical side continue to keep him in the public's minds and hearts.

Glossary

ancestral Something belonging to previous generations of someone's family.

aristocratic Something usually belonging to noble or wealthy families.

captor A person that holds someone prisoner.

dandy A man who is very concerned with his elegant appearance.

deceitfulness Deceiving or misleading someone.

descendant A person related to someone who lived in the past.

folklorist Someone who studies traditional stories and customs.

idleness Not working, producing, or in use.

illusion Something that deceives the senses or mind.

livestock Animals raised for food or other products.

metaphor A word to compare one thing to another.

misrepresent To give an inaccurate or deliberately false account of the nature of someone or something.

origin The starting point.

patron saint A saint believed to be the special guardian of a country.

primitive A member of a people who do not use or rely on complex modern technology.

retrieve To get something back.

Scandinavian Belonging to a region in northern Europe, comprising Norway, Sweden, Denmark, Finland, Iceland, and the Faroe Islands.

solitary Someone who prefers to be or live alone.

symbolism Use of images to represent something abstract with something concrete.

Vikings Scandinavian people who carried out raids and invasions on parts of Europe from the eighth to eleventh centuries CE.

wizened Looking wrinkled or shriveled.

To Learn More About Leprechauns

Books

Berresford Ellis, Peter. *The Mammoth Book of Celtic Myths and Legends*. London: Robinson, 2003.

Keightley, Thomas. *The Fairy Mythology*. London: Nabu Press, 2010.

Lover, Samuel. *Legends and Stories of Ireland*. London: Baldwin and Cradock, 1831.

McAnally, Russell R., I*rish Wonders: The Ghosts, Giants, Pookas, Demons, Leprechawns, Banshees, Fairies, Witches, Widows, Old Maids, and Other Marvels of the Emerald Isle*. New York: Houghton, Mifflin and Company, 1888.

McGarry, Mary. *Great Fairy Tales of Ireland*. London: Wolfe, 1973.

Ó hÓgáin, Dáithí. *Lore of Ireland: An Encyclopedia of Myth, Legend and Romance*. Woodbridge, England: Boydell Press, 2006.

Stewart, Bruce, (ed.) *That Other World: The Supernatural and the Fantastic in Irish Literature and Its Contexts*. Oxford, England: OUP, 1998.

Website

Celtic Folklore
www.sacred-texts.com/neu/celt
Discover ancient texts about the leprechaun and other creatures in Irish folklore.

Irish Folklore: The Truth about Leprechauns
cbladey.com/chaun/chaun.html
Explore different myths and stories connected to the leprechaun.

Bibliography

"Ancient Legends, Mystic Charms, and Superstitions of Ireland: The Leprechaun," Accessed November 23, 2014. www.sacred-texts.com/neu/celt/ali/ali021.htm.

Borges, Jorge L. *The Book of Imaginary Beings.* New York: Penguin, 1969.

Kennedy, Patrick. *Legendary Fictions of the Irish Celts.* London: Macmillan and Co., 1891.

O'Connor, Ellen. "A Few Gleanings from Tir-na-nog." *The Irish Monthly,* Vol. 41, 1913.

O'Reilly, Barry. "Now You See It, Now You Don't: Irish Legends of Buried Treasure." *Sounds from the Supernatural: Papers Presented at the Nordic-Celtic Legend Symposium.* 1994-5.

Rose, Carol. *Sprites, Fairies, Leprechauns, and Goblins.* New York: ABC-CLIO, 1998.

"Saint Patrick, Druids, Snakes, and Popular Myths." *Patheos.com.* Accessed November 23, 2014. www.patheos.com/blogs/wildhunt/2012/03/saint-patrick-druids -snakes-and-popular-myths.html.

"St. Patrick's Day: Lore of the leprechaun in Dublin." *TorontoSun.com.* Accessed November 11, 2014. www.torontosun.com/2014/03/12/st-patricks-day-lore -of-the-leprechaun-in-dublin.

Winberry, John J. "The Elusive Elf: Some Thoughts on the Nature and Origin of the Irish Leprechaun." *Folklore,* Vol. 87, 1976.

Yeats, W. B., *Fairy and Folk Tales of the Irish Peasantry.* London: Walter Scott, 1888.

Index

Page numbers in **boldface** are illustrations. Entries in **boldface** are glossary terms.

ABOUT THE AUTHOR

Katie Griffiths grew up in the county of Derbyshire, England. She studied English Literature at Edinburgh University, specializing in the power of fantasy in children's fiction. She now lives in Hangzhou, China, where she works as a teacher. In her free time, she enjoys reading, hiking, and traveling. Visit Katie online at www.katiegriffiths.net.